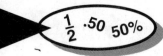

20. 0.15; 0.51; 5.01; 50.1
21. 4
22. 27
23. 21
24. 5.6
25. 0.2
26. 7.6
27. 18.7
28. 304.81
29. 1.06
30. 27.39
31. 356.14
32. $13.02
33. $163.76
34. 4,567.83

Page 27
1. 2.7
2. .14
3. 4.338
4. 1825.2
5. 4121
6. 6
7. 150.9
8. 10.625
9. 1.628
10. 31.88
11. .056
12. .00702
13. .084
14. 599.104
15. 161.505
16. 2.16408
17. 56.088
18. 48.708
19. 7.616
20. .18446
21. 1.8
22. 53
23. 145
24. .091
25. 112.34
26. .922
27. 524.75
28. 893,155
29. 0.23
30. 1679.45

Page 28
1. $93.96
2. $4.47
3. $105.30
4. $69.93
5. $53.38
6. $420.52

7. $585.39
8. $256.50
9. 2.646
10. 1.872
11. 2.6628
12. 0.00228
13. $6.30
14. 4.78
15. 137.74
16. $1.38
17. $8.37
18. .1218

Page 32
1. 5
2. 0.139
3. 10.80
4. 625
5. 0.013
6. 0.04
7. 0.03
8. 750
9. 175
10. $81.25
11. 5.7
12. .043
13. 4.9
14. 80
15. 50
16. 7/20
17. 8/125
18. 3 2/5
19. 3 1/8
20. 18 1/3
21. 4 5/8
22. 21/2500
23. 66 3/4
24. 159/500
25. 1/16
26. 4 1/4
27. 1 1/10
28. .8
29. .37 1/2 or .375
30. .66 2/3
31. .77 7/9
32. .83 1/3
33. .62 1/2 or .625
34. .33 1/3
35. .7

Page 36
1. 7%
2. 75%
3. 3.5%
4. 33 1/3%

5. 90%
6. 150%
7. .4%
8. 65%
9. 10%
10. 66 2/3%
11. .09
12. .35
13. .048
14. .22 2/9
15. .6
16. 1.25
17. .003
18. .95
19. .2
20. .33 1/3
21. 3/4
22. 2/5
23. 1/20
24. 4/5
25. 3/50
26. 9/100
27. 2/25
28. 1/5
29. 7/20
30. 43/50
31. 37.5%
32. 33 1/3%
33. 40%
34. 87.5%
35. 66 2/3%
36. 20%
37. 50%
38. 12.5%
39. 5%
40. 25%
41. 5%
42. 600%
43. 20%
44. 16 2/3%
45. 25%
46. 80
47. 90
48. 63.6
49. 130
50. 85.71

Page 39
1. $45.00
2. $45.42
3. $10.00
4. $30.00
5. $135.00
6. $73.75

7. $19.90
8. $9.12
9. $298
10. $54.08

Page 40
1. $42.29
2. $196
3. $16.20
4. $0.25
5. $1372.70

Chart
1. $\frac{1}{10}$, .10, 10%
2. $\frac{1}{4}$, .25, 25%
3. $\frac{9}{20}$, .45, 45%
4. $\frac{3}{20}$, .15, 15%
5. $\frac{4}{5}$, .80, 80%
6. $\frac{5}{6}$, .833, 83.3%
7. $\frac{77}{100}$, .77, 77%
8. $\frac{1}{20}$, .20, 20%
9. $\frac{11}{50}$, .222, 22%
10. $\frac{2}{5}$, .40, 40%

Pages 41 and 42
1. 24 pieces of pie
2. 1/4 yard
3. 4 miles
4. 1 1/8 miles
5. 2 1/2 pieces of taffy
6. 3 weeks
7. 75 ounces
8. 66 1/4 inches
9. $287.65
10. $21.79
11. $114.26
12. $81.16
13. $300; $90; $210
14. $26.45
15. 25 students
16. 150 children
17. 20 homes
18. 225 cards
19. $0.87
20. $1.50
21. 26 minutes
22. 288 boxes
23. 6 pounds
24. 6.25%

Pages 43 and 44
1. $500 every six months. Take a salary of $10,000 for Sample:
   1st year: $5,000 + $5,500 = $10,500 vs. $10,000
   2nd year: $6,000 + $6,500 = $12,500 vs. $12,000
2. about 18,000 miles
3. house numbers
4. $0.20
5. 100%
6. Choco-Chunk and Nuts to U are equal in value. Goodie Two-Shoes is the better buy.
7. 200 miles a day
8. $4,250.00
9. $1.25 to break even; $4.38 to make $25,000.
10. a. $14.00
    b. $42.00
    c. $52.50
    d. $87.50
    e. $49.00
    f. $105.00
    Yes, he saved $350.00
11. b
12. a
13. a
14. a
15. After 31 years, the system will still be worth $10!
16. 52 bushels of wheat, 55 bushels of corn, and 34 bushels of oats.

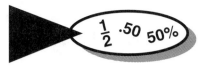

Page 8
1. 1 3/4
2. 1 4/5
3. 1 1/3
4. 1 3/5
5. 2 1/5
6. 1 3/4
7. 2 1/7
8. 2 1/5
9. 2 1/8
10. 5
11. 7/4
12. 8/5
13. 9/4
14. 23/8
15. 17/5
16. 13/3
17. 17/3
18. 23/2
19. 41/8
20. 53/12
21. 1/2
22. 2/3
23. 1/4
24. 2/3
25. 1/3
26. 6/13
27. 1/2
28. 1/3
29. 2/3
30. 1/2
31. 3/15
32. 9/12
33. 4/16
34. 6/40
35. 25/35
36. 6/36
37. 12/18
38. 10/45
39. 3/4
40. 5/7
41. 1
42. 3 1/3
43. 1 1/7
44. 4
45. 2 1/2
46. 7 2/3
47. 1 3/8
48. 25/28
49. 31/36
50. 14 1/12
51. 2
52. 1 4/5
53. 11 11/24
54. 14 16/35
55. 1 7/10

Page 11
1. 2/5
2. 1/2
3. 1/12
4. 4/7
5. 6/23
6. 1/7
7. 1/2
8. 1/15
9. 1/3
10. 5/8
11. 1/2
12. 1/8
13. 5/9
14. 7/10
15. 1/4
16. 19/30
17. 4 1/4
18. 6 15/16
19. 3 5/8
20. 9 2/7
21. 11 13/25
22. 7 1/4
23. 4 3/4
24. 24 3/17
25. 12 1/2
26. 4 2/7

Page 12
1. 3 1/4
2. 8 1/5
3. 6 7/12
4. 6 2/3
5. 3 1/2
6. 3 3/7
7. 3/10
8. 6 5/8
9. 3 7/11
10. 1 12/13
11. 2 11/12
12. 1 17/20
13. 2 13/18
14. 8 5/12
15. 10 3/4
16. 7 13/15
17. 8 5/6
18. 7 27/40

Page 15
1. 3/8
2. 2/21
3. 9/40
4. 6/35
5. 1/6
6. 1/6
7. 2/7
8. 2/9
9. 1/4
10. 3/4
11. 1/4
12. 1/6
13. 3/20
14. 35/72
15. 1/8
16. 1/10
17. 1/5
18. 2/9
19. 3/5
20. 1/2
21. 1/5
22. 2/27
23. 3/7
24. 15/154
25. 11/16
26. 1/8
27. 4/39
28. 2/7
29. 11/30
30. 4/47
31. 17/611
32. 7/4,000

Page 16
1. 1 1/4
2. 2 2/3
3. 1 1/6
4. 3 3/5
5. 1 5/7
6. 3/10
7. 6 1/8
8. 2 2/5
9. 8/9
10. 1 1/8
11. 3 1/3
12. 3 1/3
13. 5 1/3
14. 4 2/3
15. 2 2/5
16. 7/16
17. 2 1/2
18. 1 1/35
19. 1 7/18
20. 5/6
21. 8
22. 2 4/33
23. 2 2/3
24. 5 3/5
25. 9
26. 3 1/8
27. 1 121/168
28. 33/182

Page 19
1. 11/14
2. 1 13/18
3. 14/19
4. 82/87
5. 18/29
6. 1 1/4
7. 2/3
8. 5
9. 3/4
10. 3/4
11. 2 1/6
12. 3/7
13. 5/12
14. 8/9
15. 1 5/27
16. 3/10
17. 3 1/9
18. 6 1/4
19. 9 3/4
20. 1/4
21. 25/133
22. 5/64
23. 2 31/32
24. 33 3/4
25. 18/175
26. 1/32
27. 150
28. 7 1/2
29. 4 2/27
30. 10

Page 20
1. 5/6
2. 4/9
3. 15/16
4. 2 4/7
5. 2/5
6. 4
7. 1/2
8. 1
9. 4
10. 2 1/3
11. 2/9
12. 4/15
13. 4
14. 1/12
15. 7/16
16. 6 2/3
17. 2/15
18. 6
19. 10
20. 18
21. 10 1/2
22. 9 1/3
23. 12
24. 13 1/2
25. 10 2/3
26. 7
27. 4 4/5
28. 3 1/3
29. 7 1/2
30. 7/20
31. 4 2/3
32. 9
33. 1 5/6
34. 1 1/4
35. 1

Page 24
1. nine tenths
2. three hundred six thousandths
3. forty-two thousandths
4. six and three hundredths
5. eighty and seven tenths
6. two hundred thirty-four and six hundred twelve thousandths
7. sixty-eight and thirty-five ten thousandths
8. one thousand two hundred thirty-four ten thousandths
9. one and two hundred thirty-four thousandths
10. twelve and thirty-four hundredths
11. .43
12. 40.03
13. .017
14. 86.6
15. .0508
16. 5.04
17. 12.140; 12.404; 12.444; 12,400
18. 0.96; 0.9666; 10.96; 109.6
19. 0.055; 0.5; 0.505; 0.55

Editor
Gisela Lee

Editorial Manager
Karen J. Goldfluss, M.S. Ed.

Editor-in-Chief
Sharon Coan, M.S. Ed.

Cover Artist
Jessica Orlando

Art Coordinator
Denice Adorno

Creative Director
Elayne Roberts

Imaging
James Edward Grace

Product Manager
Phil Garcia

Acknowledgements
Word® software is © 1983–2000 Microsoft Corporation. All rights reserved. Word is a registered trademark of Microsoft Corporation.

Publisher
Mary D. Smith, M.S. Ed.

How to Work with
Fractions,
Decimals & Percents

Grades 5–8

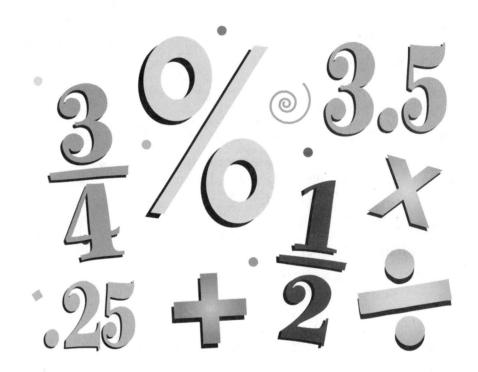

Author

Charles Shields

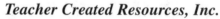

Teacher Created Resources, Inc.
6421 Industry Way
Westminster, CA 92683
www.teachercreated.com

©2000 Teacher Created Resources, Inc.
Reprinted, 2006
Made in U.S.A.

ISBN-1-57690-956-5

Teacher Created Resources

Table of Contents

A Note to Teachers and Parents

Welcome to the "How to" math series! You have chosen one of over two dozen books designed to give your children the information and practice they need to acquire important concepts in specific areas of math. The goal of the "How to" math books is to give children an extra boost as they work toward mastery of the math skills established by the National Council of Teachers of Mathematics (NCTM) and outlined in grade-level scope and sequence guidelines.

The design of this book is intended to be used by teachers or parents for a variety of purposes and needs. Each of the units contains one or more "How to" pages and one or more practice pages. The "How to" section of each unit precedes the practice pages and provides needed information such as a concept or math rule review, important terms and formulas to remember, and/or step-by-step guidelines necessary for using the practice pages. While most "How to" pages are written for direct use by the children, in some lower-grade-level books these pages are presented as instructional pages or direct lessons to be used by a teacher or parent prior to introducing the practice pages.

About This Book

The activities in this book will help your children learn new skills or reinforce skills already learned in the following areas:

- developing concepts of fractions, mixed numbers, decimals, and percents
- developing number sense for fractions and decimals
- using models to relate fractions to decimals and to find equivalent fractions
- using models to explore operations with fractions, decimals, and percents
- applying fractions, decimals, and percents to problem situations

Fractions, decimals, and percents are an important extension of children's understanding of numbers. With these concepts in hand, children are prepared for the next step: applying fractions, decimals, and percents to real-world phenomena involving measurement, probability, and statistics.

How to Work with Fractions, Decimals, & Percents: Grades 5–8 presents a comprehensive, step-by-step overview of these fundamental mathematical concepts with clear, simple, readable instructional activities. The 12 units in this book can be used in whole-class instruction with the teacher or by a parent assisting his or her child with the concepts and exercises.

This book also lends itself to use by small groups doing remedial or review work on fractions, decimals, and percents or for children and small groups in earlier grades engaged in enrichment or advanced work. Finally, this book can be used in a learning center with materials specified for each unit of instruction.

If children have difficulty on a specific concept or unit in this book, review the material and allow them to redo pages that are difficult for them. Since step-by-step concept development is essential, it's best not to skip sections of the book. Even if children find a unit easy, mastering the problems will build their confidence as they approach more difficult concepts.

Make available simple manipulatives to reinforce concepts. Use pennies, buttons, a ruler, beans, and similar materials to show proportions and ratios. Many children can grasp a numerical concept much more easily if they see it demonstrated.

This book is designed to match the standards of the National Council of Teachers of Mathematics. The standards strongly support the learning of fractions, decimals, and percents, and other basic processes in the context of problem solving and real-world applications. Use every opportunity to have students apply these new skills in classroom situations and at home. This will reinforce the value of the skill as well as the process. This book matches a number of NCTM standards including these main topics and specific features.

Concepts of Fractions, Mixed Numbers, Decimals, and Percents

Understanding the relationship between mixed numbers, decimals, and percents is a key step toward understanding more advanced concepts. This book carefully develops the step-by-step processes for renaming improper fractions as mixed numbers, for instance, or renaming fractions as decimals and percents. In addition, word problems involving practical applications of these concepts reinforce them.

Number Sense for Fractions, Decimals, and Percents

Learning numbers and their meaning in concrete, physical ways is emphasized in this book. Many examples involve determining parts of whole objects, or a percentage of time or money, for example, for the purpose of relating basic arithmetic operations to real-world problems.

Relating Fractions to Decimals and Finding Equivalencies

Students need to know how fractions, decimals, and percents relate to other numbers and concepts. Many times in this book, students will learn how to express amounts in several ways, all of which represent equivalent amounts. As a result, students will learn how to approach a problem from more than one way.

Mathematical Connections Among Fractions, Decimals, and Percents

The instructions in this book emphasize the connections among ideas in mathematics. Illustrations reinforce that a portion of an amount may be expressed or determined in several ways without sacrificing accuracy.

Problem Solving with Fractions, Decimals, and Percents

Many times in this book, a concept will be introduced first as a practical problem: calculating 6 months simple interest on $500 at 7 percent. The skills students learn through these examples are further elaborated on in the word-problem section. Students will find that their confidence in recognizing essential information in problem solving grows stronger.

Other Standards

This book aligns well with other standards which focus on teaching computational skills, such as division and multiplication, within the context of measurement and geometry. Students are also encouraged to use estimation to determine the reasonable accuracy of an answer, a skill often called for on standardized tests.

Facts to Know

A *fraction* is a part of something. A foot is a fraction of a yard. Fifty cents is a fraction of a dollar. The two numbers in a fraction are called the *numerator* (how many parts you have) and the *denominator* (how many parts in the whole).

There are two important uses of fractions—to compare the sizes of two things and to show the part of the whole.

Proper and Improper Fractions and Mixed Numbers

There are three forms of fractions.

- **Proper fraction**—a fraction in which the numerator is less than the denominator. The value of a proper fraction is always less than one whole.

  Examples: $\frac{2}{3}$ $\frac{9}{10}$ $\frac{5}{7}$ $\frac{11}{15}$

- **Improper fraction**—a fraction in which the numerator is equal to or more than the denominator. The value of an improper fraction is either equal to one or more than one.

  Examples: $\frac{5}{2}$ $\frac{7}{4}$ $\frac{12}{12}$ $\frac{80}{49}$

- **Mixed number**—a whole number and a fraction written side by side.

  Examples: $3\frac{3}{4}$ $5\frac{1}{8}$ $2\frac{1}{3}$ $10\frac{1}{6}$

Changing Improper Fractions to Mixed Numbers

The number $1\frac{1}{2}$ is made up of two parts: 1—a whole number and $\frac{1}{2}$ —a fraction.

A whole number and fraction together are a mixed number. The number $1\frac{1}{2}$ is a mixed number. It mixes a whole number and a fraction. The line between the top and bottom of a fraction means divide.

The improper fraction $\frac{3}{2}$ means $3 \div 2$. You can change an improper fraction to a mixed number by dividing. See the sample problem below.

Sample: $\frac{3}{2} = ?$

> **Step 1** → Divide the numerator (top number) by the denominator (bottom number).
>
> **Step 2** → Place your remainder over the number you divided by (the denominator) since the remainder is still a fraction.

$$\begin{array}{r} 1 \\ 2\overline{)3} \\ \underline{-2} \\ 1 \end{array} \qquad \frac{3}{2} = 1\frac{1}{2}$$

Changing Mixed Numbers to Improper Fractions

You can change a mixed number to an improper fraction. You must multiply.

Sample: $3\frac{1}{4} = ?$

> **Step 1** → Multiply the denominator by the whole number.
>
> **Step 2** → Add the numerator to that answer.
>
> **Step 3** → Place your answer over the denominator.

$$4 \times 3 = 12$$
$$12 + 1 = 13$$
$$3\frac{1}{4} = \frac{13}{4}$$

Facts to Know *(cont.)*

Reducing Fractions to Lowest Terms (Simplest Form)

Reducing a fraction means dividing both the numerator and denominator by a number that divides into them evenly.

Sample: Reduce $\frac{6}{10}$.

Step 1 → Divide both 6 and 10 by a number that goes into them evenly. The number is 2. $\frac{6}{10} \div \frac{2}{2} = \frac{3}{5}$

Step 2 → Check to see whether another number divides evenly into the top and bottom numbers of the new fraction. No number other than one divides evenly into both the numerator and the denominator. The fraction $\frac{3}{5}$ is in simplest form.

Sometimes, however, a fraction can be reduced more than once.

Sample: Reduce $\frac{12}{36}$.

Step 1 → Divide both 12 and 36 by a number that goes into them evenly. The number is 6. $\frac{12 \div 6}{36 \div 6} = \frac{2}{6}$

Step 2 → Check to see whether another number divides evenly into both the top and bottom of the new fraction. The number 2 divides evenly into both. $\frac{2 \div 2}{6 \div 2} = \frac{1}{3}$

Step 3 → Check to see whether another number divides evenly into both the top and bottom of the new number. The fraction $\frac{1}{3}$ is reduced as far as it can be.

A fraction that is reduced as far as it can be is in its lowest terms. This means that the numerator and denominator have no common factor other than 1. This means that the fraction is in simplest form. The fraction $\frac{1}{3}$ is in simplest form.

Finding a Greatest Common Factor

When working with fractions, it is easier if you try to put a fraction into its lowest terms first. Find a number that will divide evenly into both the numerator and denominator.

Sample: Simplify $\frac{24}{32}$.

Step 1 → You can divide by 2. $\frac{24 \div 2}{32 \div 2} = \frac{12}{16}$

Step 2 → However, you can divide by 2 two more times. $\frac{12 \div 2}{16 \div 2} = \frac{6}{8}$ and then $\frac{6 \div 2}{8 \div 2} = \frac{3}{4}$

So, you could have reduced $\frac{24}{32}$ to its simplest form $\frac{3}{4}$ much faster if you had divided both 24 and 32 by its greatest common factor, 8. $\frac{24 \div 8}{32 \div 8} = \frac{3}{4}$

Facts to Know (cont.)

Raising a Fraction to Higher Terms

When adding or subtracting fractions, sometimes it's necessary to raise fractions to higher terms. This is the opposite of reducing. To raise a fraction to higher terms, multiply both the numerator and the denominator of the fraction by the same number.

Sample: Raise $\frac{3}{4}$ to 20ths.

Step 1 → Divide the old denominator into the new denominator.

$$\frac{20}{4} = 20 \div 4 = 5$$

Step 2 → Multiply both the numerator and denominator of the original fraction by 5.

$$\frac{3 \times 5}{4 \times 5} = \frac{15}{20}$$

Step 3 → Check by reducing the new fraction. The reduced answer should be the original fraction.

$$\frac{15}{20} = \frac{15 \div 5}{20 \div 5} = \frac{3}{4}$$

Adding Fractions with the Same Denominator

When the sum of an addition problem is an improper fraction, change the sum to a whole number or a mixed number.

Sample: $4\frac{8}{9} + 3\frac{4}{9} = ?$

Step 1 → Add the numerators of the fractions when the denominators are the same. **8 + 4 = 12**

Step 2 → Write the total over the denominator. $\frac{12}{9}$

Step 3 → Add the whole numbers. **4 + 3 = 7**

Step 4 → Change the improper fraction to a mixed number. $\frac{12}{9} = 1\frac{3}{9}$

Step 5 → Add the mixed number to the total of the whole numbers. $7 + 1\frac{3}{9} = 8\frac{3}{9}$

Remember, always reduce. $8\frac{3}{9} = 8\frac{1}{3}$

Adding Fractions with Different Denominators

When adding fractions with different denominators, find a common denominator.

A *common denominator* is one that can be divided evenly by all the denominators in the problem. The smallest number that can be divided evenly by the other denominators is the least common denominator, finding it saves steps in reducing.

Sample: What is $\frac{1}{2}$ pound of nuts and $\frac{3}{4}$ pound of nuts added together?

Step 1 → Find a common denominator.

Step 2 → The lowest number that can be divided evenly by both denominators 2 and 4 is 4.

Step 3 → Raise $\frac{1}{2}$ to 4ths.

Step 4 → Add the fractions with the least common denominator and change the total to a mixed number.

$$\frac{1}{2} = \frac{2}{4}$$
$$+\frac{3}{4} = \frac{3}{4}$$
$$\overline{\frac{5}{4} = 1\frac{1}{4} \text{ pounds of nuts}}$$

Directions: Change the improper fractions to mixed numbers. Remember to reduce to lowest terms.

1. $\frac{7}{4} =$ 3. $\frac{4}{3} =$ 5. $\frac{11}{5} =$ 7. $\frac{15}{7} =$ 9. $\frac{34}{16} =$

2. $\frac{9}{5} =$ 4. $\frac{8}{5} =$ 6. $\frac{14}{8} =$ 8. $\frac{22}{10} =$ 10. $\frac{40}{8} =$

Directions: Change the mixed number to an improper fraction.

11. $1\frac{3}{4} =$ 13. $2\frac{1}{4} =$ 15. $3\frac{2}{5} =$ 17. $5\frac{2}{3} =$ 19. $5\frac{1}{8} =$

12. $1\frac{3}{5} =$ 14. $2\frac{7}{8} =$ 16. $4\frac{1}{3} =$ 18. $11\frac{1}{2} =$ 20. $4\frac{5}{12} =$

Directions: Reduce the fraction to lowest terms.

21. $\frac{2}{4} =$ 23. $\frac{3}{12} =$ 25. $\frac{9}{27} =$ 27. $\frac{14}{28} =$ 29. $\frac{50}{75} =$

22. $\frac{4}{6} =$ 24. $\frac{8}{12} =$ 26. $\frac{12}{26} =$ 28. $\frac{10}{30} =$ 30. $\frac{111}{222} =$

Directions: Raise the fraction to higher terms.

31. $\frac{1}{5}$ to 15ths =   33. $\frac{2}{8}$ to 16ths =   35. $\frac{5}{7}$ to 35ths =   37. $\frac{2}{3}$ to 18ths =

32. $\frac{3}{4}$ to 12ths =   34. $\frac{3}{20}$ to 40ths =   36. $\frac{1}{6}$ to 36ths =   38. $\frac{2}{9}$ to 45ths =

Directions: Add the fractions. Remember to reduce to lowest terms.

39. $\frac{1}{4} + \frac{2}{4} =$ 41. $\frac{7}{11} + \frac{4}{11} =$ 43. $\frac{2}{7} + \frac{6}{7} =$ 45. $1\frac{5}{8} + \frac{7}{8} =$

40. $\frac{3}{7} + \frac{2}{7} =$ 42. $\frac{6}{3} + \frac{4}{3} =$ 44. $2\frac{3}{4} + \frac{5}{4} =$ 46. $2\frac{1}{3} + 4\frac{4}{3} =$

Directions: Add the fractions. Remember to find a common denominator and then reduce to lowest terms.

47. $\frac{5}{8} + \frac{3}{4} =$ 50. $6\frac{5}{8} + 7\frac{11}{24} =$ 53. $8\frac{1}{6} + 3\frac{7}{24} =$

48. $\frac{4}{7} + \frac{9}{28} =$ 51. $\frac{2}{3} + \frac{7}{12} + \frac{3}{4} =$ 54. $5\frac{6}{35} + 9\frac{2}{7} =$

49. $\frac{5}{9} + \frac{11}{36} =$ 52. $\frac{3}{5} + \frac{1}{2} + \frac{7}{10} =$ 55. $\frac{13}{20} + \frac{4}{5} + \frac{1}{4} =$

Facts to Know

Subtracting Fractions with the Same Denominators

When fractions have the same denominators, subtract the numerators only and place the total over the denominator.

Sample: From a bag that contained $\frac{7}{8}$ pound of birdseed, Margery poured $\frac{3}{8}$ of a pound into the bird feeder. How much birdseed is left?

Step 1 ➤ Subtract the numerators.		$7 - 3 = 4$
Step 2 ➤ Write the answer over the denominator.		$\frac{4}{8}$
Step 3 ➤ Reduce the final answer.		$\frac{4}{8}$ pound $= \frac{1}{2}$ pound

More on Finding Common Denominators

Sometimes you must change more than one denominator to add or subtract. For example, how would you solve this problem:

Sample: $\frac{1}{2} - \frac{1}{3} = ?$

These fractions have different denominators. You cannot subtract them, nor can only one denominator be changed because 2 won't divide into 3 evenly, and 3 won't divide into 2 evenly. Therefore, you must find a common denominator, a number that both 2 and 3 will divide into evenly.

There are three methods for finding a common denominator.

Method 1— Check the largest denominator in the problem to find out whether it can be divided evenly by the other denominator(s) in the problem.

Sample: $\frac{1}{3} - \frac{1}{6} = ?$

6 can be evenly divided by 3, so there's no need to look for another number.

$$\frac{1}{3} = \frac{2}{6}$$
$$-\frac{1}{6} = \frac{1}{6}$$
$$\frac{1}{6}$$

Method 2—Multiply the denominators together to find a common denominator.

Sample: $\frac{3}{4} - \frac{2}{3} = ?$

Step 1 ➤ Multiply the denominators. The number 12 is the common denominator.

Step 2 ➤ Raise each fraction to 12ths.

Step 3 ➤ Subtract the new fractions.

$$\frac{3}{4} = \frac{9}{12}$$
$$-\frac{2}{3} = \frac{8}{12}$$
$$\frac{1}{12}$$

Method 3—Go through the multiplication table of the largest denominator.

Sample: $\frac{5}{9} - \frac{1}{6} = ?$

Step 1 ➤ Go through the multiplication table of the largest denominator, 9.

9 x 1 = 9 which cannot be divided evenly by 6.

9 x 2 = 18 which can be divided evenly by 6 and 9.

Step 2 ➤ Raise each fraction to 18ths.

Step 3 ➤ Subtract the new fractions.

$$\frac{5}{9} = \frac{10}{18}$$
$$-\frac{1}{6} = \frac{3}{18}$$
$$\frac{7}{18}$$

Facts to Know *(cont.)*

Subtracting Fractions with Different Denominators

When subtracting fractions with different denominators, find a common denominator.

Sample: Lupe walks $\frac{1}{2}$ mile to the train. She stops for coffee at Tom's restaurant, which is $\frac{3}{8}$ mile to the train. How much further does she have to walk after Tom's?

You'll have to subtract $\frac{3}{8}$ from $\frac{1}{2}$, but they don't have common denominators.

Step 1 → Find the least common denominator. The numbers 2 and 8 both evenly divisible by 8.

Step 2 → Raise $\frac{1}{2}$ to eighths.

Step 3 → Subtract the fractions using the least common denominator.

$$\begin{array}{r} \frac{1}{2} = \frac{4}{8} \\ -\frac{3}{8} = \frac{3}{8} \\ \hline \frac{1}{8} \text{ mile} \end{array}$$

Subtracting Fractions from a Whole Number

When subtracting fractions from the whole number 1, you must change the number 1 to a fraction with the same numerator and denominator as the denominator in the fraction.

Sample: Ian took one cup of sugar from a bag. He only used $\frac{3}{4}$ cup to make ice tea. How much sugar is left?

Step 1 → Change 1 to a fraction, using the same number for the numerator and denominator as the denominator of the original fraction (1 cup = $\frac{4}{4}$ cup).

Step 2 → Subtract the fractions.

$$\begin{array}{r} 1 = \frac{4}{4} \\ -\frac{3}{4} = \frac{3}{4} \\ \hline \frac{1}{4} \text{ cup left} \end{array}$$

When subtracting a fraction from a whole number larger than 1, you must regroup.

Sample: $3 - \frac{3}{8} = ?$

Step 1 → Regroup by changing 3 to $2\frac{8}{8}$. (Remeber, $1 = \frac{8}{8}$.)

Step 2 → Subtract.

$$\begin{array}{r} 3 = 2\frac{8}{8} \\ -\frac{3}{8} = \frac{3}{8} \\ \hline 2\frac{5}{8} \end{array}$$

Subtracting Mixed Numbers

You can subtract mixed numbers provided the fractions have the same denominators.

Sample : $4\frac{1}{3} - 1\frac{3}{4} = ?$

Step 1 → Find the lowest common denominator.

Step 2 → Since you can't subtract $\frac{9}{12}$ from $\frac{4}{12}$; regroup 1 as $\frac{12}{12}$ from the 4. Add it to $\frac{4}{12}$.

Step 3 → Subtract the fractions. Then subtract the whole numbers.

$$\begin{array}{r} 4\frac{1}{3} = 4\frac{4}{12} \\ -1\frac{3}{4} = 1\frac{9}{12} \end{array} = \begin{array}{r} 3\frac{4}{12} + \frac{12}{12} \\ -1\frac{9}{12} \end{array} = \begin{array}{r} 3\frac{16}{12} \\ -1\frac{9}{12} \\ \hline 2\frac{7}{12} \end{array}$$

Directions: Subtract the fractions. Remember, to reduce the fractions to lowest terms.

1. $\dfrac{4}{5} - \dfrac{2}{5} =$

5. $\dfrac{17}{23} - \dfrac{11}{23} =$

9. $\dfrac{1}{2} - \dfrac{1}{6} =$

13. $\dfrac{5}{6} - \dfrac{5}{18} =$

2. $\dfrac{9}{10} - \dfrac{4}{10} =$

6. $\dfrac{20}{21} - \dfrac{17}{21} =$

10. $\dfrac{7}{8} - \dfrac{1}{4} =$

14. $\dfrac{19}{20} - \dfrac{1}{4} =$

3. $\dfrac{7}{12} - \dfrac{6}{12} =$

7. $\dfrac{7}{8} - \dfrac{3}{8} =$

11. $\dfrac{7}{10} - \dfrac{1}{5} =$

15. $\dfrac{3}{4} - \dfrac{1}{2} =$

4. $\dfrac{6}{7} - \dfrac{2}{7} =$

8. $\dfrac{7}{15} - \dfrac{6}{15} =$

12. $\dfrac{1}{4} - \dfrac{1}{8} =$

16. $\dfrac{13}{15} - \dfrac{7}{30} =$

Directions: Subtract the fraction from the whole number.

17. $5 - \dfrac{3}{4}$

19. $4 - \dfrac{3}{8}$

21. $12 - \dfrac{12}{25}$

23. $5 - \dfrac{1}{4}$

25. $13 - \dfrac{11}{22}$

18. $7 - \dfrac{1}{16}$

20. $10 - \dfrac{5}{7}$

22. $8 - \dfrac{9}{12}$

24. $25 - \dfrac{14}{17}$

26. $5 - \dfrac{5}{7}$

Keys to Subtracting Fractions

- If the denominators in the fractions are not alike, find the lowest common denominator.
- Regroup if a minuend (the number you subtract from) is a whole number or the fraction in a minuend is smaller than the fraction in a subtrahend (the number being subtracted).
- Subtract the fractions first and then subtract the whole numbers.

Directions: Subtract the mixed numbers. Remember, reduce to the lowest term.

1. $9\frac{7}{8}$
   $-6\frac{5}{8}$

2. $15\frac{9}{10}$
   $-7\frac{7}{10}$

3. $14\frac{19}{24}$
   $-8\frac{5}{24}$

4. $11\frac{5}{6}$
   $-5\frac{1}{6}$

5. $6\frac{7}{8}$
   $-3\frac{3}{8}$

6. 5
   $-1\frac{4}{7}$

7. 6
   $-5\frac{7}{10}$

8. 9
   $-2\frac{3}{8}$

9. 7
   $-3\frac{4}{11}$

10. $8\frac{4}{13}$
    $-6\frac{5}{13}$

11. $6\frac{1}{4}$
    $-3\frac{1}{3}$

12. $10\frac{3}{5}$
    $-8\frac{3}{4}$

13. $4\frac{2}{9}$
    $-1\frac{1}{2}$

14. $12\frac{1}{4}$
    $-3\frac{5}{6}$

15. $20\frac{5}{12}$
    $-9\frac{2}{3}$

16. $14\frac{2}{5}$
    $-6\frac{8}{15}$

17. $18\frac{1}{3}$
    $-9\frac{1}{2}$

18. $13\frac{3}{8}$
    $-5\frac{7}{10}$

Facts to Know

All fractions can be multiplied by multiplying the numerators and then multiplying the denominators. You don't need common denominators to multiply.

Sample: Andrew can jog a mile in $\frac{1}{4}$ of an hour. Lauren can run the same distance in $\frac{1}{2}$ that time. How long would it take Lauren to run a mile?

To find out, you need to multiply $\frac{1}{2}$ by $\frac{1}{4}$.

Step 1 ➡ Multiply the numerators. $1 \times 1 = 1$

Step 2 ➡ Multiply the denominators. $2 \times 4 = 8$

Step 3 ➡ Write the answer as a fraction. $\frac{1}{2} \times \frac{1}{4} = \frac{1 \times 1}{2 \times 4} = \frac{1}{8}$

Sometimes the answer to a multiplication problem can be reduced.

Sample: $\frac{3}{4} \times \frac{1}{6} = ?$

Step 1 ➡ Multiply the fractions. $\frac{3}{4} \times \frac{1}{6} = \frac{3}{24}$

Step 2 ➡ Write the fraction in simplest form by dividing the numerator and denominator by the greatest common factor, which in this case is 3. $\frac{3 \div 3}{24 \div 3} = \frac{1}{8}$

Multiplying Three Fractions

Now and then you will have to multiply three fractions together.

Sample: $\frac{2}{3} \times \frac{1}{5} \times \frac{1}{3} = ?$

Step 1 ➡ Multiply the numerators of the first two fractions. Then multiply that answer by the numerator of the third fraction.

Step 2 ➡ Multiply the denominators of the first two fractions. Then multiply that answer by the denominator of the third fraction. $\frac{2 \times 1}{3 \times 5} = \frac{2 \times 1}{15 \times 3} = \frac{2}{45}$

Step 3 ➡ Write fraction in simplest form, if possible. The fraction $\frac{2}{45}$ is reduced as far as it can be.

Facts to Know (cont.)

Canceling as a Shortcut

Sometimes the fractions in a multiplication problem can be canceled. Canceling is a shortcut to reducing. To cancel find a number that divides evenly into both the numerator and denominator of the problem.

Sample: $\frac{3}{4} \times \frac{7}{24} = ?$

Step 1 → Find a number that will divide evenly. The number 3 will divide evenly into 3 and 24.

Step 2 → Cancel 3 and 24 by 3. $3 \div 3 = 1$ $24 \div 3 = 8$

Step 3 → Multiply across by the new numbers.

Step 4 → Reduce if possible, but by canceling you already did some of the work of reducing.

$$\frac{\overset{1}{\cancel{3}}}{4} \times \frac{7}{\underset{8}{\cancel{24}}} = \frac{7}{32}$$

Multiplying Fractions and Whole Numbers

When multiplying a fraction by a whole number, turn the whole number into a fraction with a denominator of 1.

Sample: Andrew plans to sprint $\frac{3}{5}$ of a mile each day for four days in a row as part of his regular workout. How many miles will this total?

You will need to multiply $\frac{3}{5}$ by 4.

Step 1 → Write 4 as an improper fraction with a denominator of 1. $4 = \frac{4}{1}$

Step 2 → Multiply across.

Step 3 → Change the improper fraction to a whole or mixed number. $\frac{3}{5} \times \frac{4}{1} = \frac{12}{5} = 2\frac{2}{5}$

Multiplying Mixed Numbers

When multiplying mixed numbers, it is usually helpful to change the mixed number to an improper fraction.

Sample: $3\frac{2}{5} \times 4\frac{1}{3} = ?$

Step 1 → Change both mixed numbers to improper fractions. $3\frac{2}{5} = (3 \times 5) + 2 = \frac{17}{5}$

$4\frac{1}{3} = (4 \times 3) + 1 = \frac{13}{3}$

Step 2 → Multiply across the new numbers. $\frac{17}{5} \times \frac{13}{3} = \frac{221}{15}$

Step 3 → Change the improper fraction to a whole or mixed number. $\frac{221}{15} = 14\frac{11}{15}$

Directions: Multiply the fractions. Remember to write the answer in simplest form when possible.

1. $\frac{1}{2} \times \frac{3}{4} =$

2. $\frac{2}{3} \times \frac{1}{7} =$

3. $\frac{3}{8} \times \frac{3}{5} =$

4. $\frac{1}{5} \times \frac{6}{7} =$

5. $\frac{1}{2} \times \frac{1}{3} =$

6. $\frac{2}{3} \times \frac{1}{4} =$

7. $\frac{1}{3} \times \frac{6}{7} =$

8. $\frac{4}{9} \times \frac{1}{2} =$

9. $\frac{1}{2} \times \frac{1}{2} =$

10. $\frac{1}{2} \times \frac{3}{2} =$

11. $\frac{1}{3} \times \frac{3}{4} =$

12. $\frac{2}{9} \times \frac{3}{4} =$

13. $\frac{3}{8} \times \frac{2}{5} =$

14. $\frac{5}{8} \times \frac{7}{9} =$

15. $\frac{1}{2} \times \frac{1}{2} \times \frac{1}{2} =$

16. $\frac{1}{2} \times \frac{1}{4} \times \frac{4}{5} =$

17. $\frac{1}{2} \times \frac{2}{3} \times \frac{3}{5} =$

18. $\frac{5}{9} \times \frac{3}{7} \times \frac{14}{15} =$

19. $\frac{6}{7} \times \frac{7}{8} \times \frac{4}{5} =$

20. $\frac{11}{15} \times \frac{10}{11} \times \frac{3}{4} =$

21. $\frac{9}{10} \times \frac{1}{4} \times \frac{8}{9} =$

22. $\frac{5}{6} \times \frac{14}{15} \times \frac{2}{21} =$

23. $\frac{20}{21} \times \frac{9}{16} \times \frac{4}{5} =$

24. $\frac{3}{4} \times \frac{5}{7} \times \frac{2}{11} =$

25. $\frac{11}{12} \times \frac{3}{4} =$

26. $\frac{7}{8} \times \frac{2}{14} =$

27. $\frac{4}{15} \times \frac{5}{13} =$

28. $\frac{3}{5} \times \frac{10}{21} =$

29. $\frac{121}{300} \times \frac{10}{11} =$

30. $\frac{125}{470} \times \frac{320}{1000} =$

31. $\frac{289}{1222} \times \frac{2}{17} =$

32. $\frac{14}{525} \times \frac{15}{320} =$

Directions: Multiply the fractions and whole numbers. Use canceling whenever you can.

1. $\frac{1}{4} \times 5 =$ 5. $\frac{2}{7} \times 6 =$ 9. $\frac{2}{9} \times 4 =$ 13. $8 \times \frac{2}{3} =$

2. $4 \times \frac{2}{3} =$ 6. $\frac{1}{10} \times 3 =$ 10. $\frac{3}{8} \times 3 =$ 14. $7 \times \frac{2}{3} =$

3. $\frac{1}{6} \times 7 =$ 7. $\frac{7}{8} \times 7 =$ 11. $5 \times \frac{2}{3} =$ 15. $4 \times \frac{3}{5} =$

4. $6 \times \frac{3}{5} =$ 8. $3 \times \frac{4}{5} =$ 12. $\frac{2}{3} \times 5 =$ 16. $\frac{7}{8} \times \frac{1}{2} =$

Directions: Multiply the mixed numbers. Use canceling whenever you can.

17. $3\frac{3}{4} \times \frac{2}{3} =$ 21. $2\frac{4}{7} \times 3\frac{1}{9} =$ 25. $1\frac{5}{16} \times 2\frac{6}{7} \times 2\frac{2}{5} =$

18. $3\frac{3}{7} \times \frac{3}{10} =$ 22. $1\frac{9}{11} \times 1\frac{1}{6} =$ 26. $1\frac{7}{8} \times \frac{3}{4} \times 2\frac{2}{9} =$

19. $\frac{5}{8} \times 2\frac{2}{9} =$ 23. $1\frac{5}{9} \times 1\frac{5}{7} =$ 27. $2\frac{5}{6} \times \frac{1}{7} \times 4\frac{1}{4} =$

20. $\frac{8}{15} \times 1\frac{9}{16} =$ 24. $2\frac{5}{8} \times 2\frac{2}{15} =$ 28. $8\frac{2}{8} \times \frac{2}{13} \times \frac{1}{7} =$

Facts to Know

The key to dividing with fractions is understanding reciprocals. A *reciprocal* is two numbers that have the product of 1. Here are some examples:

Samples
$\frac{2}{3}$ and $\frac{3}{2}$ are reciprocals because $\frac{2}{3} \times \frac{3}{2} = \frac{6}{6}$ or 1
$\frac{4}{1}$ and $\frac{1}{4}$ are reciprocals because $\frac{4}{1} \times \frac{1}{4} = \frac{4}{4}$ or 1

Knowing what a reciprocal is will be your key to understanding how to divide with fractions.

Dividing Fractions by Fractions

Dividing a number by 2 gives the same answer as multiplying by $\frac{1}{2}$. For example, $6 \div 2 = 3$ just as $6 \times \frac{1}{2} = 3$.

The answers are the same. The reciprocal of $\frac{2}{1}$ is $\frac{1}{2}$. Turning a fraction upside down is called *inverting*.

To divide by a fraction, invert the fraction you are dividing by and then multiply.

Sample: Let's say you're building a kite, and you have a piece of string $\frac{3}{4}$ yard long. Into how many $\frac{3}{8}$ yard pieces can you snip the string? The problem looks like this: $\frac{3}{4} \div \frac{3}{8} = ?$

Step 1 → Invert the fraction you are dividing by. $\frac{3}{8}$ inverted is $\frac{8}{3}$.

Step 2 → Multiply across. $\frac{3}{4} \div \frac{3}{8} = \frac{3}{4} \times \frac{8}{3} = \frac{24}{12}$

Step 3 → Reduce or change an improper fraction to a mixed or whole number, if possible. $\frac{24}{12} = $ **2 pieces of string**

The fraction to invert is always the fraction to the right of the division sign.

Facts to Know *(cont.)*

Canceling in Dividing Fractions

Sometimes you can cancel in division. Invert before you cancel and multiply after you cancel.

Sample: $\frac{1}{3} \div \frac{1}{6} = ?$

    Step 1 ⟶ Invert and change to multiplication. $\frac{1}{3} \div \frac{1}{6} = \frac{1}{3} \times \frac{6}{1}$

    Step 2 ⟶ 3 is a factor of 3 and 6. Cancel and divide the numerator and denominator by 3. $\frac{1}{3} \times \frac{6}{1}$

    Step 3 ⟶ Multiply. $\frac{1}{\cancel{3}} \times \frac{\cancel{6}^{2}}{1} = \frac{2}{1} = 2$

Dividing a Fraction by a Whole Number

When dividing a fraction by a whole number, first change the whole number to a fraction with a denominator of 1.

Sample: Suppose a recipe calls for dividing $\frac{1}{2}$ pound of butter into four equal parts.

Hint: You must divide $\frac{1}{2}$ by 4.

    Step 1 ⟶ Change the whole number, 4, to a fraction. $4 = \frac{4}{1}$

    Step 2 ⟶ Invert the divisor. $\frac{4}{1}$ **inverted is** $\frac{1}{4}$

    Step 3 ⟶ Multiply. $\frac{1}{2} \times \frac{1}{4} = \frac{1}{8}$ pound of butter.

Dividing a Whole Number by a Fraction

Sometimes the whole number is not the number you are dividing by—it is the number being divided.

Sample: Divide 4 pounds of candy into bags holding $\frac{1}{2}$ pound each.

Hint: You must divide 4 by $\frac{1}{2}$.

    Step 1 ⟶ Change the whole number to a fraction. $4 = \frac{4}{1}$

    Step 2 ⟶ Invert the divisor. (Invert the number to the right of the division sign.) $\frac{1}{2}$ **inverted is** $\frac{2}{1}$

    Step 3 ⟶ Multiply. $4 \div \frac{1}{2} = \frac{4}{1} \times \frac{2}{1} = \frac{8}{1}$ **or 8 bags**

Dividing and Mixed Numbers

Before dividing, change any mixed numbers to improper fractions.

Sample: $1\frac{1}{4} \div \frac{2}{3} = ?$

    Step 1 ⟶ Change the mixed number to an improper fraction. $1\frac{1}{4} = \frac{5}{4}$

    Step 2 ⟶ Invert and multiply. $\frac{5}{4} \times \frac{3}{2} = \frac{15}{8} = 1\frac{7}{8}$

Directions: Divide the fractions below.

1. $3\frac{2}{3} \div 4\frac{2}{3} =$

2. $4\frac{3}{7} \div 2\frac{4}{7} =$

3. $2\frac{1}{3} \div 3\frac{1}{6} =$

4. $5\frac{6}{7} \div 6\frac{3}{14} =$

5. $3\frac{3}{5} \div 5\frac{4}{5} =$

6. $\frac{5}{6} \div \frac{2}{3} =$

7. $\frac{1}{4} \div \frac{3}{8} =$

8. $\frac{5}{12} \div \frac{2}{24} =$

9. $\frac{3}{10} \div \frac{12}{30} =$

10. $\frac{1}{5} \div \frac{4}{15} =$

11. $\frac{13}{20} \div \frac{3}{10} =$

12. $\frac{2}{7} \div \frac{2}{3} =$

13. $\frac{1}{6} \div \frac{2}{5} =$

14. $\frac{4}{9} \div \frac{1}{2} =$

15. $\frac{8}{9} \div \frac{3}{4} =$

16. $\frac{3}{6} \div 1\frac{2}{3} =$

17. $2\frac{1}{3} \div \frac{3}{4} =$

18. $3\frac{3}{4} \div \frac{3}{5} =$

19. $6\frac{1}{2} \div \frac{2}{3} =$

20. $1\frac{1}{2} \div 6 =$

21. $\frac{5}{7} \div 3\frac{4}{5} =$

22. $\frac{1}{4} \div 3\frac{1}{5} =$

23. $2\frac{3}{8} \div \frac{4}{5} =$

24. $3\frac{3}{4} \div \frac{1}{9} =$

25. $\frac{2}{5} \div 3\frac{8}{9} =$

26. $\frac{3}{8} \div 12 =$

27. $15 \div \frac{1}{10} =$

28. $2\frac{3}{6} \div \frac{1}{3} =$

29. $3\frac{2}{3} \div \frac{9}{10} =$

30. $2\frac{1}{2} \div \frac{1}{4} =$

Directions: Divide the fractions, whole numbers, or mixed numbers. Reduce when possible.

1. $\frac{1}{2} \div \frac{3}{5} =$

10. $\frac{7}{9} \div \frac{1}{3} =$

19. $8 \div \frac{4}{5} =$

28. $2\frac{1}{2} \div \frac{3}{4} =$

2. $\frac{1}{3} \div \frac{3}{4} =$

11. $\frac{2}{3} \div 3 =$

20. $12 \div \frac{2}{3} =$

29. $1\frac{1}{2} \div \frac{1}{5} =$

3. $\frac{3}{4} \div \frac{4}{5} =$

12. $\frac{4}{5} \div 3 =$

21. $9 \div \frac{6}{7} =$

30. $\frac{2}{5} \div 1\frac{1}{7} =$

4. $\frac{6}{7} \div \frac{1}{3} =$

13. $2 \div \frac{1}{2} =$

22. $7 \div \frac{3}{4} =$

31. $3\frac{1}{2} \div \frac{3}{4} =$

5. $\frac{1}{5} \div \frac{1}{2} =$

14. $\frac{1}{6} \div 2 =$

23. $10 \div \frac{5}{6} =$

32. $2\frac{1}{4} \div \frac{1}{4} =$

6. $\frac{1}{2} \div \frac{1}{8} =$

15. $\frac{7}{8} \div 2 =$

24. $6 \div \frac{4}{9}$

33. $5\frac{1}{2} \div 3 =$

7. $\frac{3}{8} \div \frac{3}{4} =$

16. $4 \div \frac{3}{5} =$

25. $4 \div \frac{3}{8} =$

34. $3\frac{1}{8} \div 2\frac{1}{2} =$

8. $\frac{1}{4} \div \frac{1}{4} =$

17. $\frac{2}{3} \div 5 =$

26. $1\frac{3}{4} \div \frac{1}{4} =$

35. $3\frac{3}{4} \div 3\frac{3}{4} =$

9. $\frac{4}{5} \div \frac{1}{5} =$

18. $4 \div \frac{2}{3} =$

27. $8 \div 1\frac{2}{3} =$

Facts to Know

What Is a Decimal?

Decimals are kinds of fractions. Twenty-five cents, written as $0.25, is a decimal, and as $\frac{25}{100}$, a fraction which represents twenty-five hundredths (or if you reduce it, $\frac{1}{4}$ of a dollar).

The name of a decimal is determined by the number of places to the right of the decimal point.

Number of Places	Decimal Name	Example	Proper Fraction
one place	tenths	.7 (seven tenths)	$\frac{7}{10}$
two places	hundredths	.05 (five hundredths)	$\frac{5}{100}$
three places	thousandths	.016 (sixteen thousandths)	$\frac{16}{1000}$
four places	ten-thousandths	.0054 (fifty-four ten-thousandths)	$\frac{54}{10000}$

The decimal point separates the whole-number places from the places less than one.

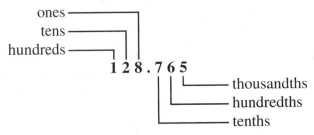

Mixed decimals are numbers with both whole numbers and decimals.

Reading Decimals

To read a decimal correctly, first find the decimal point. Whole numbers are to the left of the decimal point; any numbers to the right of the decimal point form a decimal fraction. Say "and" for the decimal point.

"thirty and seven thousandths" **30.007**

Comparing Decimal Values

When comparing decimal values, give each decimal the same number of places.

Sample: Which is larger—.15 or .3?

Step 1 ⟶ Give the decimals the same number of places. Add a zero to the .3. **.3** ⟶ **.30**

Step 2 ⟶ Now compare .15 and .30. Both decimals have two places, or hundredths. $\frac{30}{100}$ is larger than $\frac{15}{100}$.

So .3 is larger than .15. Notice that the zero added to the .3 did not change its position in the tenths place. The zero was added just to make the comparison easier to see.

Facts to Know *(cont.)*

Changing Decimals to Fractions

When writing a decimal as a fraction, write the numbers as the numerator of the fraction. Write the number of places in the decimal as the denominator.

Sample: Change .05 to a common fraction and reduce.

Step 1 ➝ Write 5 as the numerator. Don't write the zero because it has no value. $\underline{5}$

Step 2 ➝ Two decimal places are hundredths. Write 100 as the denominator. $\frac{5}{100}$

Step 3 ➝ Reduce $\frac{5}{100}$ by 5. $\frac{5}{100} = \frac{1}{20}$

Sample: Change 7.8 to a mixed number and reduce.

Step 1 ➝ Write 7 as a whole number and 8 as the numerator of the fraction. $7\,\underline{8}$

Step 2 ➝ One decimal place is tenths. Write 10 as the denominator. $7\frac{8}{10}$

Step 3 ➝ Reduce $\frac{8}{10}$ by 2. $7\frac{8}{10} = 7\frac{4}{5}$

Changing Fractions to Decimals

In a fraction, the line separating the numerator from the denominator means "divided by." When changing a common fraction to a decimal, divide the numerator by the denominator. Place a decimal point and zeros—one or two—to the right of the numerator in the division problem.

Sample: Change $\frac{2}{25}$ to a decimal.

Step 1 ➝ Divide 2 by 25.

Step 2 ➝ Place a decimal point and two zeros to the right of 2. One zero is not enough because 20 is not divisible by 25.

$$25\overline{)\begin{array}{l}.08\\2.00\\\underline{2\,00}\\0\end{array}}$$

Step 3 ➝ Divide and bring the decimal point up into the answer.

Sample: Change $\frac{2}{9}$ to a decimal.

Step 1 ➝ Divide 2 by 9.

Step 2 ➝ Place a decimal point and two zeros to the right of 2.

Step 3 ➝ Divide and bring the decimal point up into the answer. After two decimal places, write the remainder as a fraction over the number you divided by.

$$9\overline{)\begin{array}{l}.22\frac{2}{9}\\2.00\\\underline{-1.8}\!\downarrow\\20\\\underline{-18}\\2\end{array}}$$

Facts to Know (cont.)

Rounding Decimals

When rounding decimals, if the number to the right of the place being rounded is 5 or larger, round up by 1 and drop the remaining numbers. If the number to the right of the place being rounded is less than 5, drop the remaining numbers.

    Sample: Round $8.476 to the nearest cent.

        Step 1 → Keep in mind that cents refers to hundredths and includes the first two decimal places. In this case, 7 is the last number of cents.

        Step 2 → The number to the right of the cents is 6. Since 6 is greater than 5, add 1 hundredth to $8.47 and drop the 6. The answer is $8.48.

Adding Decimal Numbers

Add decimals the way you would whole numbers, but make sure to line up the decimal points. Second, place a decimal point under all the other decimal points.

Sample

$.43 + .20 + .12 = ?$

$$
\begin{array}{r}
.43 \\
.20 \\
+ .12 \\
\hline
.75
\end{array}
$$

Sample

$.6 + .07 + .713 = ?$

$$
\begin{array}{r}
.600 \\
.070 \\
+ .713 \\
\hline
1.383
\end{array}
$$

The zeros in second sample above are just placeholders. They don't change the value of the decimals. The idea is just to make the addition easier to see.

Regrouping when Adding Decimal Numbers

Regroup numbers in decimal addition just the way you do with whole numbers.

$$
\begin{array}{r}
1 \\
8.395 \\
+ .243 \\
\hline
8.638
\end{array}
$$

Subtracting Decimal Numbers

Subtract decimals the way you would whole numbers, but make sure to line up the decimal points. Second, place a decimal point under all the other decimal points.

Sample

$.43 - .22 = ?$

$$
\begin{array}{r}
.43 \\
- .22 \\
\hline
.21
\end{array}
$$

Sample

$55.534 - .41 = ?$

$$
\begin{array}{r}
55.534 \\
- .410 \\
\hline
55.124
\end{array}
$$

Regrouping when Subtracting Decimal Numbers

As in subtracting whole numbers, sometimes you need to regroup. Regroup money amounts in the same way.

$$
\begin{array}{r}
4\ 12 \\
48.5\!\!\not{5}\!\not{2} \\
- 23.23 \\
\hline
25.29
\end{array}
$$

Directions: Write the following numbers in words.

1. .9 _____
2. .306 _____
3. .042 _____
4. 6.03 _____
5. 80.7 _____

6. 234.612 _____
7. 68.0035 _____
8. .1234 _____
9. 1.234 _____
10. 12.34 _____

Directions: Change the words below into numbers.

11. forty-three hundredths

_____

12. forty and three hundredths

_____

13. seventeen thousandths

_____

14. eighty-six and six tenths

_____

15. five hundred eight ten thousandths

_____

16. five and four hundredths

_____

Directions: List in order from least to greatest.

17. 12.444; 12.140; 12.404; 12,400

_____

18. 0.96; 10.96; 0.9666; 109.6

_____

19. 0.5; 0.55; 0.505; 0.055

_____

20. 5.01; 50.1; 0.51; 0.15

_____

Directions: For problems 21–23, round to the nearest whole number. For problems 24–27, round to the nearest tenth. For problems 28–30, round to the nearest hundredth.

21. 3.75 _____
22. 26.8 _____
23. 21.04 _____
24. 5.62 _____

25. 0.183 _____
26. 7.601 _____
27. 18.718 _____
28. 304.8146 _____

29. 1.059 _____
30. 27.389 _____

Directions: Add or subtract the decimal amounts.

31.
```
   57.86
   98.37
   46.31
   70.63
 + 82.97
```

32.
```
   $3.16
   $8.48
   $0.65
 + $0.73
```

33.
```
   $275.58
 − $111.82
```

34.
```
   4,782.72
 −  214.89
```

Facts to Know

You multiply decimals the same way you multiply whole numbers. Also, the decimal points do not have to be lined up. However, you must be careful to correctly place the decimal point in the product for multiplication. The number of decimal places in the answer must equal the total number of places to the right of the decimal point in the problem.

Decimal Points in the Final Answer

Multiplying decimals is the same as multiplying whole numbers. The key is to count the decimal places in each factor.

Sample: 458 x 7.3 = ?

    Step 1 ⟶ Line up the digits.

    Step 2 ⟶ Multiply as with whole numbers.

    Step 3 ⟶ Count the decimal places in each
                  factor. The product must have
                  an equal number of decimal
                  places as the problem.

$$\begin{array}{r} 45\,8 \\ \times\ 7.3 \\ \hline 1374 \\ +\ 32060 \\ \hline 3{,}343.4 \end{array}$$

Zero as a Place Holder

Remember, the product has the same number of decimal
places as the factors. Sometimes you have to add zeros as needed.

$$\begin{array}{r} 21.45 \\ \times\ 0.0321 \\ \hline 2145 \\ 42900 \\ +\ 643500 \\ \hline 0.688545 \end{array}$$

Multiplying Decimals by Whole Numbers

When multiplying decimals by whole numbers, counting off decimal places is the key.

Sample: One inch contains 2.54 centimeters. How many centimeters are there in four inches?

You must multiply the number of centimeters in one inch by four.

    Step 1 ⟶ Line up the numbers for easy multiplication. You don't need to line up the
               decimal points, however.

    Step 2 ⟶ Multiply the numbers as you would multiply whole numbers.

    Step 3 ⟶ Count the number of decimal places in both numbers that you multiplied. Make
               sure the decimal places in the product equal the number of decimal places in the
               problem.

$$\begin{array}{rl} 2.54 & \text{(2 decimal places)} \\ \times\quad 4 & \text{(0 decimal places)} \\ \hline 10.16 & \text{(2 decimal places)} \end{array}$$

So the final answer is 10.16 cm

Facts to Know *(cont.)*

Multiplying Decimals by Decimals

When multiplying decimals by decimals, counting off decimal places is the key again.

Sample: John can run 4.30 miles in an hour during an ultramarathon. How far does he run in 7.5 hours?

You must multiply the distance John runs in an hour by 7.5.

Step 1 ➤ Line up the numbers for easy multiplication. You don't need to line up the decimal points, however.

Step 2 ➤ Multiply the numbers as you would multiply whole numbers.

Step 3 ➤ Count the number of decimal places in both numbers that you multiplied. Make sure the decimal places in the product equal the number of decimal places in the problem.

$$
\begin{array}{r}
4.30 \quad \text{(2 decimal places)} \\
\underline{\times\ 7.5} \quad \text{(1 decimal place)} \\
2150 \\
\underline{+\ 30100} \\
32.250 \quad \text{(3 decimal places)}
\end{array}
$$

We can drop the final zero to make the answer easier to read. So the final answer is 32.25 miles.

Multiplying Decimals by 10, 100, and 1000

When you multiply by powers of 10, do the following:

Multiply by 10 ⟶ Move the decimal point 1 place to the *right*. ⟶ **3.63 x 10 = 36.3**

Multiply by 100 ⟶ Move the decimal point 2 places to the *right*. ⟶ **3.63 x 100 = 363.**

Multiply by 1000 ⟶ Move the decimal point 3 places to the *right*. ⟶ **3.63 x 1000 = 3,630.**

Multiplying Money

Amounts of money are multiplied the same way other decimal numbers are multiplied. The number of decimal places in the answer must equal the number of decimal places in the problem.

Sample

$$
\begin{array}{r}
\$155.73 \quad \text{(2 decimal places)} \\
\underline{\times\ 31} \\
\$4{,}827.63 \quad \text{(2 decimal places)}
\end{array}
$$

Directions: Multiply the decimals by whole numbers.

1. 9 x .3 = _____

2. 4 x .035 = _____

3. 482 x .009 = _____

4. 45.63 x 40 = _____

5. 634 x 6.5 = _____

6. .75 x 8 = _____

7. 50.3 x 3 = _____

8. 2.125 x 5 = _____

9. .814 x 2 = _____

10. 15.94 x 2 = _____

Directions: Multiply the decimals by decimals.

11. .08 x .7 = _____

12. .234 x .03 = _____

13. .14 x .6 = _____

14. 73.6 x 8.14 = _____

15. 43.65 x 3.7 = _____

16. 4.26 x .508 = _____

17. 1.23 x 45.6 = _____

18. 29.7 x 1.64 = _____

19. 19.04 x .4 = _____

20. .802 x .23 = _____

Directions: Multiply the decimals by 10, 100, and 1000.

21. .180 x 10 = _____

22. .53 x 100 = _____

23. .145 x 1000 = _____

24. .00091 x 100 = _____

25. 11.234 x 10 = _____

26. .00922 x 100 = _____

27. 52.475 x 10 = _____

28. 893.155 x 1000 = _____

29. .00023 x 1000 = _____

30. 167.945 x 10 = _____

Keys to Multiplying Decimals

- Line up the numbers. You don't need to line up the decimal points, however.
- Multiply the numbers as you would multiply whole numbers.
- Count the number of decimal places in both numbers that are being multiplied. Make sure the decimal places in the product equal the number of decimal places in the problem.

Directions: Multiply to solve each problem.

1. $46.98
    x   2

2. $1.49
    x   3

3. $21.06
    x   5

4. $9.99
    x   7

5. $1.57
    x   34

6. $105.13
    x   4

7. $45.03
    x   13

8. $17.10
    x   15

9. 0.84
    x 3.15

10. 2.08
    x 0.9

11. 0.28
    x 9.51

12. 0.0076
    x 0.30

13. $10.50
    x 0.60

14. 47.8
    x 0.1

15. 14.2
    x 9.7

16. $5.75
    x 0.24

17. $5.58
    x 1.5

18. 0.14
    x 0.87

Facts to Know

Take a look at these two division problems and notice the difference.

$$3 \overline{)6}^{\,2} \qquad 3 \overline{).6}^{\,.2}$$

In the first problem, a whole number is being divided into a whole number. In the second, a whole number is being divided into a decimal. Notice that the decimal point is placed directly above in the quotient.

In fact, dividing decimals by whole numbers is simple if you place the decimal point in the quotient first.

Sample: 5.95 ÷ 7 = ?

Step 1 ➝ Place the decimal point in the quotient.
Step 2 ➝ Divide as with whole numbers.

$$\begin{array}{r} 0.85 \\ 7{\overline{)5.95}} \\ -5\,6\!\downarrow \\ \hline 35 \\ -35 \end{array}$$

Multiplying Decimals by 10, 100, and 1000

When you multiply by powers of 10, do the following:

Divide by 10 ⟶	Move the decimal point 1 place to the *left*. ⟶	**3.63 ÷ 10 = 0.363**
Divide by 100 ⟶	Move the decimal point 2 places to the *left*. ⟶	**3.63 ÷ 100 = 0.0363**
Divide by 1000 ⟶	Move the decimal point 3 places to the *left*. ⟶	**3.63 ÷ 1000 = 0.00363**

Zeros as Placeholders

When you cannot divide, use zeros to hold the decimal point.

Sample: .410 ÷ 5 = ?

In your first step, you cannot divide 5 into 4, so place a zero above the 4. It serves as a placeholder. Don't move the decimal point. Next divide 5 into 41 and complete the problem.

$$\begin{array}{r} .082 \\ 5{\overline{).410}} \\ -40\!\downarrow \\ \hline 10 \\ -10 \\ \hline 0 \end{array}$$

Adding Zeros Inside the Division Box

Sometimes you cannot divide without adding zeros to the dividend (the number being divided). You can add as many zeros as you need after the decimal point without changing the value of the number.

Sample: 3 ÷ 6 = ?

Step 1 ➝ 6 will not divide into 3. Add a decimal point and a zero after the 3.

Step 2 ➝ Place the decimal point in the quotient now, so you don't forget.

Step 3 ➝ Divide 30 by 6, which is 5. Place the 5 after the decimal point, just as you put a zero after the decimal point in the problem.

$$6{\overline{)3}} \quad \longrightarrow \quad 6{\overline{)3.0}} \quad \longrightarrow \quad \begin{array}{r} .5 \\ 6{\overline{)3.0}} \\ -3\,0 \\ \hline 0 \end{array}$$

Facts to Know *(cont.)*

Dividing Decimals by Decimals

Dividing decimals by decimals means you must move the decimal point by changing the decimal number to a whole number. Multiply the divisor (the dividing number) and the dividend (the number being divided) by the same power of 10. This will make the divisor a whole number.

Sample: $2.6\overline{)20.8}$

Step 1 → The divisor has sixth tenths. Multiply the divisor and the dividend by 10 to get a whole number divisor. What you do to the divisor number, you must do to the dividend.

$$2.6\overline{)20.8} \longrightarrow \begin{array}{r} 8 \\ 26\overline{)208} \\ -208 \\ \hline 0 \end{array}$$

Step 2 → Divide 208 by 26, which is 8.

Note: If the divisor has hundredths, move the decimal point 2 places. If the divisor has thousandths, move the decimal 3 places.

More About Adding Zeros Inside the Division Box

You can make a divisor that is a decimal into a whole number by moving the decimal. To do so, you may need to add zeros to the dividend.

Sample: $3.15\overline{)6.3}$

Step 1 → 3.15 has hundredths. Change 3.15 to the whole number 315 by moving the decimal 2 places. Remember, that you must do to the dividend what you did to the divisor. However, you must add a zero to the dividend as a placeholder in order to move the decimal 2 places.

$$3.15\overline{)6.3}$$

$$\begin{array}{r} 2 \\ 315\overline{)630} \\ -630 \\ \hline 0 \end{array}$$

Step 2 → Divide 630 by 315, which is 2.

Sometimes, you need to add more than one zero to the dividend, depending on how many places you move the decimal in the divisor.

Dividing Money

Money is divided in the same way as other decimals. Add a dollar sign and put the decimal point in the quotient directly above the one in the dividend. Look at the sample on the right.

$$\begin{array}{r} \$0.30 \\ 6\overline{)\$1.80} \\ -18 \\ \hline 0 \end{array}$$

Facts to Know (cont.)
Changing Fractions to Decimals

To change fractions into decimals, divide the numerator by the denominator.

Sample: Change $\frac{3}{4}$ to a decimal.

Step 1 ➤ Set up the division problem. Divide the numerator 3 by the denominator 4.

Step 2 ➤ Notice that you must add a zero because 3 is not divisible by 4 unless you do. Place the decimal point in the quotient now, so you don't forget.

Step 3 ➤ Divide 3.0 by 4, which is 0.75.

$$
\begin{array}{r}
0.75 \\
4\overline{)3.00} \\
-2\,8\downarrow \\
\hline
20 \\
-20 \\
\hline
0
\end{array}
$$

Sometimes you must add several zeros to the dividend. If the answer has a remainder and a number turns into a repeating decimal, such as $.33\overline{3}$, write the remainder in fraction form—$.33\frac{1}{3}$.

Changing Mixed Numbers to Decimals

To change a mixed number to a decimal number, work with only the fraction first. You can include the whole number in your answer.

Sample: Change $2\frac{6}{7}$ to a decimal.

Step 1 ➤ Set up the division problem. Divide 6, the numerator of the fraction, by the denominator 7.

Step 2 ➤ Notice that you must add a zero. The number 6 isn't divisible by 7 unless you do. Place the decimal point in the quotient now, so you don't forget.

$$
\begin{array}{r}
0.85\frac{5}{7} \\
7\overline{)6.00} \\
-5\,6\downarrow \\
\hline
40 \\
-35 \\
\hline
5
\end{array}
$$

Step 3 ➤ Divide 6.0 by 7. Add another zero. Turn the remainder into a fraction.

Step 4 ➤ Add the whole number to the answer. The final answer is $2.85\frac{5}{7}$

Changing Decimals to Fractions

To change a decimal into a fraction, do the following three things:

Step 1 ➤ Drop the decimal point and place the number into the numerator of a fraction.

Step 2 ➤ Make the the denominator a 1 followed by as many zeros as there were decimal places.

$$.35 = \frac{35}{100}$$

Step 3 ➤ Reduce the fraction if you can.

$$.007 = \frac{7}{1000}$$

Directions: Solve the division problems.

1. $\dfrac{.7}{.14} =$
6. $\dfrac{9.2}{230} =$
11. $\dfrac{45.6}{8} =$

2. $\dfrac{6}{43.2} =$
7. $\dfrac{.8}{27.2} =$
12. $\dfrac{.258}{6} =$

3. $\dfrac{4}{.3704} =$
8. $\dfrac{\$30}{.04} =$
13. $\dfrac{3.43}{.7} =$

4. $\dfrac{3.}{.0048} =$
9. $\dfrac{\$42}{.24} =$
14. $\dfrac{7.2}{.09} =$

5. $\dfrac{.8}{60} =$
10. $\$65 \div \dfrac{4}{5} =$
15. $\dfrac{60}{1.2} =$

Directions: Change each decimal to a fraction or a mixed number. Reduce to the lowest terms.

16. .35 =
20. 18.33 =
24. .318 =

17. .064 =
21. 4.625 =
25. .0625 =

18. 3.4 =
22. .0084 =
26. 4.25 =

19. 3.125 =
23. 66.75 =
27. 1.10 =

Directions: Change each fraction to a decimal.

28. $\dfrac{4}{5} =$
30. $\dfrac{2}{3} =$
32. $\dfrac{5}{6} =$
34. $\dfrac{1}{3} =$

29. $\dfrac{3}{8} =$
31. $\dfrac{7}{9} =$
33. $\dfrac{5}{8} =$
35. $\dfrac{7}{10} =$

Facts to Know

What Is a Percent?

Percent means "per hundred." The symbol % also means percent or "per hundred." Percent is a business term going back to the Roman times which is still used to measure interest rates, commission rates, mark-ups, discounts, and tax rates.

Percent is another way of writing a fraction with a denominator of 100. You can see how decimals, fractions, and percents are three ways of saying the same amount:

$$0.30 \longrightarrow \text{say, "thirty hundredths"}$$

$$\frac{30}{100} \longrightarrow \text{say, "thirty hundredths"}$$

$$30\% \longrightarrow \text{say, "thirty percent," which means "thirty per hundred"}$$

Changing Decimals to Percents

To change a decimal to a percent, move the decimal point two places to the right and write a % sign.

Sample: Change .16 to a percent   **.16 = .16 = 16%**

No need to put the decimal point to the right of a whole number.

Sample: Change .4 to a percent   **.4 = .40 = 40%**

You need to add a zero in order to move the decimal point two places.

Sample: Change .015 to a percent.   **.015 = .01 5 = 1.5%**

Moving the decimal two places puts it in the middle of 15.

Sample: Change $.16\frac{2}{3}$ to a percent. $.16\frac{2}{3} = .16\frac{2}{3} = 16\frac{2}{3}\%$

You don't need to put the decimal point between the whole number and the fraction.

Changing Percents to Decimals

To change percents to decimals, do the reverse of what you did with the decimal point in changing decimals to percents—move it to the left.

Sample: Change 6% to a decimal. $6\% = .06 = .06$

Step 1 ▶ Remove the % sign.

Step 2 ▶ Move the decimal point 2 places to the left. If you don't see a decimal point, there is an imaginary one to the right of the number.

Step 3 ▶ Place zeros in front if necessary.

No matter how many places there are in a number, the rule is the same about moving the decimal.

Samples: 300% = 300. or 3   175% = 175. =

Facts to Know (cont.)

Fractional Percents

A fractional percent is a number such as $\frac{1}{3}\%$ or $\frac{1}{5}\%$. First change the fraction to a decimal (See Unit 7). Then follow the same steps for changing a percent to a decimal.

$$\frac{1}{3}\% = .3\% = .003$$

$$\frac{1}{5}\% = .20\% = .0020$$

Changing Percents to Fractions

To change a percent to a fraction, follow these steps:

Sample: Change 30% to a fraction.

> **Step 1** ⟶ Remove the percent sign. $30\% \longrightarrow 30$

> **Step 2** ⟶ Make the number the numerator of the fraction. $30 \longrightarrow \underline{30}$

> **Step 3** ⟶ Write 100 for the denominator. $\frac{30}{100}$

> **Step 4** ⟶ Simplify the fraction, if possible. $\frac{30}{100} = \frac{3}{10}$

Changing Fractions to Percents

To change a fraction to a percent, follow these steps:

Sample: Change $\frac{5}{8}$ to a percent.

> **Step 1** ⟶ Change the fraction to a decimal. Divide the numerator 5 by the denominator 8.

> **Step 2** ⟶ Follow the rules for changing a decimal to a percent.

$$\frac{5}{8} = 8\overline{)5.000} \quad .625 = 62.5\%$$
$$\frac{-\ 4\ 8\downarrow}{\quad 20\ |}$$
$$\frac{-\ 16\downarrow}{\quad\ 40}$$
$$\frac{-\ 40}{}$$

Finding a Percent of a Number

To find a percent of a number, change the percent to a fraction or a decimal and multiply.

Sample: Your teacher says that only 4% of two classes totaling 50 students will be awarded tickets to a baseball game. How many students will receive tickets?

You want to find 4% or $\frac{4}{100}$ of 50.

> **Step 1** ⟶ Change 4% to a fraction or to a decimal.

> **Step 2** ⟶ Multiply 50 by the fraction $\frac{4}{100}$ or the decimal .04.

As a fraction ⟶ $4\% = \frac{4}{100}$

(or)

As a decimal ⟶ $4\% = .04$

The final answer is 2 tickets because 4% of 50 is 2.

$$\frac{4}{100} \times \frac{50}{1} = \frac{200}{100} = 2 \text{ or } .04 \times 50 = 2$$

Facts to Know (cont.)

Finding a Percent of a Number and Rounding

Percent is often used in connection with money, but money in the United States has only two decimal places. When a money answer has more than two decimal places, round off the answer to the nearest cent.

Sample: Find 12% of $14.70.

Step 1 ⟶ Change 12% to a decimal. 12% = .12

Step 2 ⟶ Multiply $14.70 by .12.

Step 3 ⟶ Round to the nearest cent.

$$\begin{array}{r} \$14.70 \\ \times\ \ .12 \\ \hline 2940 \\ +\ 14700 \\ \hline \$1.7640 = \$\ 1.76 \end{array}$$

Since 4 is in the thousandths place and is less than 5, drop it for the final answer. If the number in the thousandths place were 5 or greater than 5, you would raise the number in the hundredths place.

Finding What Percent One Number Is of Another

To find what percent one number is of another, make a fraction by placing the part—usually the smaller number— over the whole, which is usually the larger number.

Sample: What percent is 15 of 40?

Step 1 ⟶ Place the part over the whole and reduce. $\frac{15}{40} = \frac{3}{8}$

Step 2 ⟶ Change the fraction to a percent.

$$\frac{15}{40} = \frac{3}{8} \times \frac{100}{1} = \frac{300}{8} = \frac{75}{2} = 37\frac{1}{2}\ \%$$

Finding a Number When a Percent of It Is Given

Sometimes you know only the percent of a number that is missing. To find the missing number, change the percent to a fraction or a decimal. Then divide the amount you have by the fraction or decimal.

Sample: The student government of the junior high had a car wash and raised $525. That is 75% of what they need to purchase a sound system for the cafeteria. How much do they need?

Step 1 ⟶ Change 75% to a fraction or change 75% to a decimal.　　$75\% = \frac{75}{100} = \frac{3}{4}$

$75\% = .75$

Step 2 ⟶ Divide $525 by the fraction or divide $525 by the decimal.

$$\$525 \div \frac{3}{4} = \frac{\overset{175}{\cancel{\$525}}}{1} \times \frac{4}{\underset{1}{\cancel{3}}} = \$700 \quad \text{or} \quad .75\overline{)\,\$525.00\,}\ \overset{\$700}{\underset{\underline{-525}}{}}\ 0$$

Directions: Change the decimals to percents.

1. .07 = _____
2. .75 = _____
3. .035 = _____
4. $.33\frac{1}{3}$ = _____
5. .9 = _____

6. 1.5 = _____
7. .004 = _____
8. .65 = _____
9. .1 = _____
10. $.66\frac{2}{3}$ = _____

Directions: Change the percents to decimals.

11. 9% = _____
12. 35% = _____
13. 4.8% = _____
14. 22 2/9% = _____
15. 60% = _____

16. 125% = _____
17. .3% = _____
18. 95% = _____
19. 20% = _____
20. 33 1/3% = _____

Directions: Change the percents to fractions.

21. 75% = _____
22. 40% = _____
23. 5% = _____
24. 80% = _____
25. 6% = _____

26. 9% = _____
27. 8% = _____
28. 20% = _____
29. 35% = _____
30. 86% = _____

Directions: Change the fractions to percents.

31. $\frac{3}{8}$ = _____
32. $\frac{1}{3}$ = _____
33. $\frac{2}{5}$ = _____
34. $\frac{7}{8}$ = _____
35. $\frac{2}{3}$ = _____

36. $\frac{1}{5}$ = _____
37. $\frac{1}{2}$ = _____
38. $\frac{1}{8}$ = _____
39. $\frac{1}{20}$ = _____
40. $\frac{1}{4}$ = _____

Directions: Find the percent of a number.

41. 17 is what percent of 340? _____
42. 420 is what percent of 70? _____
43. 60 is what percent of 300? _____
44. 25 is what percent of 150? _____
45. 30 is what percent of 120? _____

Directions: Find the number when the percent is given.

46. 16 is 20% of what number? _____
47. 63 is 70% of what number? _____
48. 70 is 110% of what number? _____
49. 13 is 10% of what number? _____
50. 12 is 14% of what number? _____

Facts to Know

When money is borrowed, you must pay to use it because someone else is losing an opportunity to use it while you have it. What you pay to use the money is called *interest*. The rate of interest is a percent. The money you borrow is called the *principal*. Simple interest is paid only on the principal.

The Interest Formula

To calculate the amount of simple interest on a loan, use this formula:

Interest = Principal x Rate of Interest x Time (or) I = PRT

Rate of Interest

The rate of interest is always given as a percent. You often see rates of interest on loans and investments posted outside of banks.

Time

Time in connection with loans is always expressed in years or parts of a year.

$$1 \text{ month} = \frac{1}{12} \text{ of a year} \qquad\qquad 6 \text{ months} = \frac{6}{12} \text{ or } \frac{1}{2} \text{ year}$$

Calculating Interest

To find simple interest, use the formula **I = PRT**

> **Sample:** How much would a loan of $500 be at 6% interest for 6 months?

> > **Step 1** ➤ Use the interest formula. The formula to calculate interest is this:
> > **Interest = Principal x Rate of Interest x Time (I = P x R x T)**

> > **Step 2** ➤ Change the rate, given as a percent, to a fraction and reduce. Set up time as a fraction of a year.

$$R = \frac{6}{100} = \frac{3}{50}$$

$$T = \frac{6}{12} = \frac{1}{2}$$

> **Step 3** ➤ Multiply *principal* x *rate* x *time*. Cancel where possible.

$$I = \frac{\overset{\overset{5}{\cancel{10}}}{\cancel{500}}}{1} \times \frac{3}{\cancel{50}} \times \frac{1}{\underset{1}{\cancel{2}}} = \$15$$

You can also change the percent to a decimal (6% = .06) and the time to a decimal (6 months = $\frac{6}{12}$ = .5) and then multiply.

I = $500.00 x .06 x .5 = $15

Facts to Know (cont.)

Calculating Interest (cont.)

Sample: A T-shirt costs $24.99 and a pair of jeans costs $34.99. Each is on sale for 25% off the original price. If Jenna bought the T-shirt and jeans while they were on sale, what was her total price before adding tax? What is the total amount that Jenna had to pay for her purchase after tax was added? (Tax is 8%.)

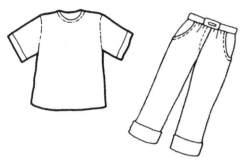

$24.99   original T-shirt price
x 0.25   discount
$6.2475 = $6.25 (rounded to the nearest hundredth)

$24.99
– $6.25
$18.74   sale price for T-shirt

$34.99   original jeans price
x 0.25   discount
$8.7475 = $8.75 (rounded to the nearest hundredth)

$34.99
– $8.75
$26.24   sale price for jeans

Jenna paid $18.74 + $26.24 = $44.98 for the T-shirt and jeans.

Discounts and Sales

A *discount* is used by manufacturers and merchants to mean taking off a certain percentage of the price given in a price list. This price is called the *list price*. The list price less the discount is known as the *net price*. The noun "discount" can be used as a verb, too—"We're discounting by 15% the list price on all new cars and trucks during our storewide 'Get into Spring' sale!"

You would ask "What's the discount?" but not, "What's the sale?" Often you have to figure out your own savings during a sale, and this is where understanding decimals and percents comes in handy.

Let's say, for instance, you read that a local amusement park is offering a single, one-day pass to all rides for $12.50, or a special two-day pass for $20.00. You do some quick decimal arithmetic.

$12.50
x   2   one-day pass
$25.00

So your savings on a two day pass is the following:

$25.00   one-day pass
– $20.00   two-day pass
$5.00

But, just curious—what percent off is that?

$$\frac{\$5.00}{\$25.00} = \frac{x}{100} \longrightarrow \text{invert and multiply} \quad \frac{\$5.00}{\$25.00} \times \frac{100}{x} = \frac{500}{25} \text{ or } 20\% \text{ off}$$

Directions: Calculate the simple interest.

Cost: $500.00

Annual Rate of Interest: 9%

1. Interest paid annually _____

2. 12 equal payments to pay the loan plus the interest _____

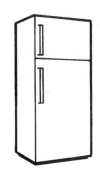

Cost: $160.00

Bi-annual Rate of Interest: 12.5%

3. Interest paid in six months _____

4. 6 equal payments to pay the loan plus the interest _____

Cost: $750.00

Annual Rate of Interest: 18%

5. Interest paid in one year _____

6. 12 equal payments to pay the loan plus the interest _____

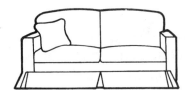

Cost: $199.00

Annual Rate of Interest: 5%

7. Interest paid over two years _____

8. 24 equal payments to pay the loan plus the interest _____

Cost: $1,000.00

Annual Rate of Interest: 14.9%

9. Interest paid over two years _____

10. 24 equal payments to pay the loan plus the interest _____

Calculating Fractions, Decimals, and Percents

Directions: Some states require that out-of-state businesses pay a shipping tax to send goods to state residents. Refer to this table to do the problems below. (**Note:** The shipping rates do not reflect the actual current rates.)

Some States' Shipping Taxes		
Alabama . . . . AL 8.00%		
Maryland . . . . MD 5.75%		
Georgia . . . . GA 4.00%		
Illinois . . . . IL 2.00%		
Indiana . . . . IN 5.00%		
Kentucky . . . . KY 6.00%		
Missouri . . . . MO 5.725%		

1. Miguel lives in Maryland and purchased a sweater for $39.99 from a catalog. Add the shipping tax. What's the total cost of the sweater? _____

2. Mr. and Mrs. Wong paid a total of $200.00 for an entertainment center for their home in Chicago, Illinois. The salesperson said that there was already a 2% shipping tax already added to the final price. What was the price of the entertainment center before the tax was added? _____

3. Stuart lives in Alabama and recently joined a book club that will send a book to him every month. The books are $15.00 each. The book club billing will include the shipping tax. What is the total amount that Stuart will have to pay for each book? _____

4. The Middlebury High School band in Indiana is going to sell holiday ornaments to raise money for uniforms. Each ornament will cost $5.00. How much is the shipping price per ornament? _____

5. The Williams family live in Lexington, Kentucky. They recently purchased a computer for $1,295.00. What is the total price for the computer after the shipping tax was added? _____

Directions: Complete the table below.

	Fraction	Decimal	Percent
1.	$\frac{1}{10}$		
2.		.25	
3.			45%
4.			15%
5.	$\frac{4}{5}$		
6.	$\frac{5}{6}$		
7.		.77	
8.	$\frac{1}{20}$		
9.		.222	
10.			40%

Directions: Solve the word problems.

1. James Hart Junior High is having a bake sale. Mrs. Nichols brought 3 pies and cut them into eighths. How many pieces of pie did she have to sell? _____

2. Dave worked over July 4th on his deck. He cut a board $1\frac{1}{4}$ yards long into 5 equal pieces. How many yards long was each piece? _____

3. The Park Forest Running and Pancake Club jogged 18 miles in $4\frac{1}{2}$ hours. How many miles did they jog per hour? _____

4. Lupe bicycles to work. She bicycled a total of $3\frac{3}{8}$ miles to work in 9 days. How many miles did she bicycle in 3 days? _____

5. Tiffany works in a candy shop. She made $\frac{5}{8}$ feet of taffy. She needs to cut it into $\frac{1}{4}$ foot pieces. How many pieces will she get? _____

6. On his summer diet, Gilbert lost $5\frac{2}{3}$ pounds. His doctor's chart showed he lost $1\frac{8}{9}$ pounds per week. How many weeks did it take him to lose the $5\frac{2}{3}$ pounds? _____

7. If a small glass of tomato juice weighs $3\frac{3}{4}$ ounces, how many ounces will 20 glasses weigh? _____

8. Mindy was $62\frac{1}{2}$ inches tall last fall. She grew $3\frac{3}{4}$ inches since then. How many inches tall is she now? _____

9. You have $237.65 in the bank and your grandmother gives you $50 for your birthday. How much money do you have now? _____

10. If diesel fuel costs $1.238 a gallon, find the cost of 17.6 gallons. (Round to the nearest cent.) _____

11. Manuel bought a used jeep for $5,484.48. He has to pay for it in 48 equal monthly payments. How much will each payment be? _____

12. Bob's gross pay for bagging groceries at Rudy's Supermarket is $92.31 a week. His deductions are federal income tax: $8.82; state income tax: $0.55; social security: $1.41; and health insurance, $0.37. What is Bob's net pay on Friday night? _____

13. Mrs. Anderson's Girl Scout troop has $600 in savings. The girls collected 50% of the money by recycling aluminum cans, 15% of the money came from donations and 35% of it came from their annual auction. How much money was raised by recycling cans? _____ donations? _____ by having an auction? _____

14. Your purchases total $24.95. If the sales tax rate is 6%, what is the total amount that you must pay? (round up to the nearest penny) _____

15. On Monday, 100 students arrived on two buses. On Tuesday, many students had the flu, and only 75% of Monday's group arrived at school. How many students had the flu? _____

16. Two hundred and fifty people are expected to turn out for the 4th of July picnic. Sixty percent of them will be children. How many children are expected to attend? _____

17. Four hundred new homes are being built in the town of Frankfort, and only 5% have swimming pools. How many have swimming pools? _____

18. Marco had 300 trading cards. His friend, Juan, told Marco he will give him 75% more. How many cards is Juan going to give to Marco? _____

19. Johnson's Drugs has penny candy. Ian purchased $0.65 of taffy and $0.20 for root beer barrels. There is a $0.02 sales tax. How much does he pay? _____

20. A round-trip subway train ticket costs $0.55. A 20-trip pass costs $9.50. If you took 20 trips, how much did you save by buying the pass? _____

21. On a cell phone, there is a charge of $0.03 per minute. How many minutes can you talk for $0.78? _____

22. A big shipment of computer parts arrived at Don's Computer World. It weighed 360 pounds. Inside the shipment, each box weighed 1.25 pounds. How many boxes were in the shipment? _____

23. At $0.17 per pound, how many pounds of gumdrops can you buy for $1.02? _____

24. Eli painted $\frac{1}{16}$ of the living room wall and stopped when the phone rang. What percent of the wall did he paint? _____

Directions: Do these brain teasers in small groups or pairs. Use paper and pencil to draw out your ideas or make your calculations.

1. Mike started a new job in March. Which would be better: an annual pay raise of $2,000 or a raise of $500 every six months? _____

2. If a piece of paper is 0.0001 inch thick, how tall of a pile would it make if the number of papers were doubled 50 times? _____

3. Mr. Burton went to the hardware store. "How much are these?" he asked the clerk. "$0.25 each," came the reply. "OK, I'll take 100," Mr. Burton said. He paid only $0.75. What did he buy? _____

4. "Summertime Fun Juice" comes in a returnable bottle for $1.60. The juice costs $1.20 more than the bottle. You can return the empty bottle for a refund. How much should you receive? _____

5. In Justin, Minnesota, 90% of the people drink coffee and 80% drink tea. Also, 70% drink apple juice and 60% drink orange juice. None of the people drink all four beverages, but they all drink three of the four. What percent of them drink juice? _____

6. Little Bobby Jenks compared candy bars. Choco-Chunk was 50% more expensive than Goodie Two-Shoes and contained 20% less weight than Nuts to U. However, Nuts to U was 50% heavier than Goodie Two-Shoes and cost 25% more than Choco-Chunk. Which is the best buy? _____

7. Ajax car rental charges $35.00 per day and $0.45 per mile to rent their cars. How many miles can you drive and still keep the cost under $125.00 per day? _____

8. At Dorothy's Drapes, a saleswoman is paid a salary of $300.00 plus a 40% sales commission. How much does she have to sell to make $2,000.00? _____

9. Hometown wants to hold a fundraiser for a new auditorium. A band called the Rave-Ups, offers to give one concert for $10,000 and 20% of the ticket receipts. About 10,000 teenagers will attend. What admission price will Hometown have to charge just to break even? _____ What admission price would Hometown have to charge to earn a profit of $25,000? _____

Summer Camp Save-Up

10. Hal wants to attend camp in Troy, Wisconsin. He needs to have $350.00 to pay his way for two weeks. He has started mowing lawns and saving money. Fill in each blank.

    a. The first week he saved 4% of his goal: _____

    b. The second week he saved 12% of his goal: _____

    c. The third week he saved 15% of his goal: _____

    d. The fourth week he saved 25% of his goal: _____

    e. The fifth week he saved 14% of his goal: _____

    f. The sixth week he saved 30% of his goal: _____

    Was Hal able to pay his way to summer camp? _____

Super Savings

Big Deal Shields's Warehouse of Super Savings lets you make the choice. For everything being sold, you can choose one of two ways to save money on the deal.

11. **table: $199.00**

    Which is the better deal? _____

    a. $50.00 off purchases of $100.00 or more

    b. 35% off any purchase

13. **apples: $0.89 per lb.**

    Which is the better deal? _____

    a. Buy 1 lb, get a second free

    b. Big sale—$0.48 per lb.

12. **telephone: $49.99**

    Which is the better deal? _____

    a. Get $15.00 back in company rebate

    b. Save 20% on any sporting equipment

14. **television: $150.00**

    Which is the better deal? _____

    a. Sale—40% off

    b. $50.00 off any purchase

15. Jack purchased a new computer system for $10,000. It loses 20% of its value every year. The first year it will be worth $2,000 less, the second year $1,600 less and so on. How many years will it take for the computer system to be worth $10? _____

16. A farmer took 141 bushels of three different grains to the market and received $565.00 for all of it. His wheat sold for $5.00 a bushel, corn for $4.00, and oats for $2.50. How many bushels of each did he take to market? _____

Directions: Using your computer skills, plan a real or imaginary fun day of activities and calculate the cost. The following directions were written specifically for *Microsoft Word*® but can be modified to be used with any similar word-processing software.

1. Open a new *Word* document.

2. Click on the **Center** button on the **Formatting Toolbar.** Set the font size to 24 or 25 points. Type of the title of your fun day.

3. Reset the font size to 12 or 14 points. Press the **Enter** or **Return** key twice. Click on the **Align Left** button. Type a paragraph describing the planned activities for your fun day. Press the **Enter** or Return key twice.

4. From the **View** menu, select the **Page Layout** if it is not already selected.

5. From the **TABLE** menu, select **Insert Table.** In the dialogue box that pops up, type in 2 for the number of columns and your predetermined number of rows. Select **Auto** for the column width and then click **OK**.

6. Click in the first cell in the left column. Type one item or activity. Click in the first cell in the right column. Type the cost of the first item and activity.

7. If you need to adjust a column width, move the cursor over the vertical line of the column. When the cursor changes to a resizing arrow, click and drag the line to the left or right.

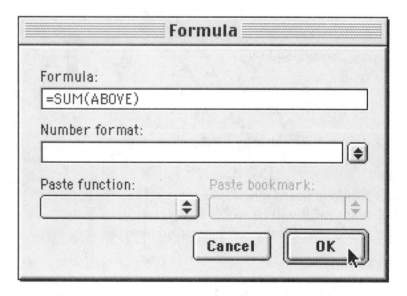

8. Finish filling in the items or activities in the left column and their costs in the right column.

9. In the last cell in the left column, type "Total Costs".

10. Click in the last cell in the right column. From the **TABLE** menu, select **Formula.** In the dialogue box that pops up, "=SUM(ABOVE)" will appear by default. Click **OK**.

11. Save and print your document.

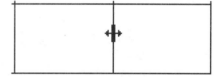

Sample

A Day at an Amusement Park

I would like to go to the amusement park. At the park, I will ride the roller coaster. I will eat a corn dog and popcorn. I will play a tossing game.

Park admission	$5
Roller coaster	$1.50
Corn dog	$2
Popcorn	$0.75
Tossing game	$1.00
Total costs	$10.25